I0821864

Bees

Leo Statts

abdopublishing.com

Printed in the United States of America, North Mankato, Minnesota
042017
092017

Cover Photo: iStockphoto
Interior Photos: iStockphoto, 1, 5 (top), 5 (bottom), 7, 8, 9, 10–11, 13, 14–15, 17, 19; Kenn Clark/iStockphoto, 6; Red Line Editorial, 11, 20 (left), 20 (right), 21 (left), 21 (right); Rainer Merk/iStockphoto, 12; Muhammad Naaim/ Shutterstock Images, 18

Editor: Brienna Rossiter
Series Designer: Madeline Berger
Art Direction: Dorothy Toth

Publishers Cataloging-in-Publication Data
Names: Statts, Leo, author.
Title: Bees / by Leo Statts.
Description: Minneapolis, MN : Abdo Zoom, 2018. | Series: Backyard animals | Includes bibliographical references and index.
Identifiers: LCCN 2017931132 | ISBN 9781532120015 (lib. bdg.) | ISBN 9781614797128 (ebook) | ISBN 9781614797685 (Read-to-me ebook)
Subjects: LCSH: Bees--Juvenile literature. | Insects--Juvenile literature.
Classification: DDC 595.79--dc23
LC record available at http://lccn.loc.gov/2017931132

Table of Contents

Bees

Bees are insects. There are many kinds of bees.

Honeybees are well-known.

So are bumblebees.

All bees have six legs and four wings. Bees are known for their sting.

But only female bees
have stingers.

Body

Bees have three main body parts. They have a head, a **thorax**, and an **abdomen**.

They also have two **antennae**.

Habitat

Bees live almost all over the world. You can even find them in your backyard. They carry **pollen** from flower to flower.

Where bees live

Food

Bees have a special tongue.

It looks like a straw. They use it to suck **nectar** from flowers.

Some bees use the nectar to make honey. They store it in honeycomb. They can eat it later.

Life Cycle

Some bees live in nests called hives. One female bee is the queen. She lays the eggs. The other bees help take care of the hive.

Male bees only live a few years.

Females live longer. A queen bee can live up to five years.

Average Size – Largest

A Chalicodoma pluto bee is larger than a penny.

Average Size – Smallest

A Perdita minima bee is smaller than a penny.

Glossary

abdomen - the back part of an insect's body.

antennae - the two long, thin body parts on an insect's head.

nectar - a sweet liquid that flowering plants make.

pollen - the tiny, yellow grains of flowers.

thorax - the middle part of an insect's body.

Booklinks

For more information on bees, please visit abdobooklinks.com

Learn even more with the Abdo Zoom Animals database. Check out abdozoom.com for more information.

Index